THE FEARFUL CHILD

THE FEARFUL CHILD

Poems by
CAROL FROST

Ithaca House

ACKNOWLEDGEMENTS

Many of these poems were first published in the following magazines: *The American Poetry Review*, *The Kenyon Review*, *Poetry NOW*, *Shenandoah*, *The Virginia Quarterly Review*, *Prairie Schooner*, *New England Review*, *Northwest Review*, *Mademoiselle*, *Pequod*, *The Agni Review*, *Cincinnati Poetry Review*, *The Chariton Review*, *Montana Review*, *The Laurel Review*, *Nebraska Review*, *Cimarron Review*, *raccoon*, *Gramercy Review*, *Bits*, *Dacotah Territory*, and *Chiaroscuro*.

A few of these poems were included in the chapbook *Cold Frame* (Owl Creek Press, 1982). Thanks to Rich Ives and Laurie Blauner.

Cover drawing by Cora Cohen.

I want to thank the National Endowment for the Arts for a fellowship in 1981-82 and the Corporation of Yaddo for residencies during which much of this book was written.

Copyright 1983, by Carol Frost
All rights reserved.

Ithaca House
108 North Plain Street
Ithaca, New York 14850

Library of Congress Cataloging in Publication Data

Frost, Carol, 1948-
    The fearful child.

    I. Title.
PS3556.R596F4   1983   811'.54   82-25861
ISBN 0-87886-121-1

Contents

THE FAIRY TALE	*1*
THE HAIRCUT	*2*
THE UNDRESSING	*3*
THE SCAR	*4*
THE FEARFUL CHILD	*6*
THE HERON	*8*
AUTUMN APOLOGY	*10*
AUBADE OF AN EARLY HOMO SAPIENS	*11*
STAGS AND SALMON	*12*
THE LIGHT ASKS	*13*
THE NEW DOG: VARIATIONS ON A TEXT BY JULES LAFORGUE	*15*
PACKING MOTHER'S THINGS	*17*
FOR THE INFANT WHOSE HEART STOPPED FOR ELEVEN MINUTES	*18*
UNFINISHED SONG	*19*
OLD CAT	*20*
AN ADOLESCENT GIRL	*21*
COUNTRY MARRIAGE	*22*
PASSAGE	*24*
OUR NIGHT	*25*
TWO POEMS / TOWARD SILENCE	*26*
FROST	*28*
DEATH IN WINTER	*29*
THE CEMETERY IS EMPTY	*30*
THE GARDEN	*31*
THE EMBROIDERY	*32*
THE WINTER WITHOUT SNOW	*33*
A GOOD CAFETERIA	*34*
THE SECRET	*35*
THE DAUGHTER	*36*

THREE APPARITIONS	*37*
INFLUENZA	*40*
A RED NIGHTGOWN	*41*
WHAT WILL BECOME OF THE FAT AND SLOW PERFORMING WOMAN?	*42*
SOMETIMES WE SAY IT IS LOVE	*43*
TO FISH	*44*
COLD FRAME	*46*
HIS MIND CEASES	*48*
PRAYER FOR MY SON	*49*
THE DAY OF THE BODY	
IF A MODEL	*50*
SHE THINKS OF LOVE	*51*
THE MAN AND THE WOMAN	*52*
SO WHEN HE LEAVES	*53*
WHERE ARE YOU GOING?	*54*
NO BATTER	*55*
ODE TO THE HORSESHOE CRAB	*57*
CONSTELLATION	*58*
THE HOMEMADE PIANO	*59*
AFTERWORD	

for my friends

*En haut de la route, pres d'un bois de lauriers,
je l'ai entouree avec ses voiles amassees, et
j'ai senti un peu son immense corps. L'aube
et l'enfant tomberent au bas du bois.*

RIMBAUD

The Fairy Tale

In the clearing it's growing dark.
The fattening goats are sleepy.
Soon light on the raspberry bushes goes out,
and the women bending down in their gardens
again and again to set a fresh world
go on home.
In the dark, entangled wood
is a cabin and a lover at the piano
playing the songs of Brahms.
As if with hands over eyes,
someone enters the purple wood
to find the path half-blown away
by the night's breezes.
With the heart of a phantom
she nears the faint illume of the door
and goes in. The piano is silent.
In the clearing,
laughing and laughing at the moon,
a goat bites through his rope
and heads toward the garden.

The Haircut

When the boy's head is heavy with his own secret
cap of hair, his mother calls him to her,
asking him to tell her about his day.
When last she called him from the depths
of the wood and combed with slender fingers
the golden current of his hair, the white
of his hidden brow, like a headstone,
had made her almost cry.
After she cut his hair, his head was quick
as a deer turning in a field to face new danger.
By the light raining down in a field in August's waste,
by the antique vase about to be knocked over
by his child's elbow, by her own perfume
lasting in the room after they leave,
can she explain her pity for him,
his forehead full of blond mysteries?

The Undressing

They took off their clothes 1000 nights
and felt the plaster of the moon
sift over them, and the ground roll
them in its dream. Little did they know
the light and clay and their own sweat
became a skin they couldn't wash away.
Each night bonded to the next,
and they grew stiffer. They noticed this
in sunlight—there were calluses,
round tough moons on their extremities,
shadows under their eyes,
and sometimes a sour smell
they hadn't had as children.
It worried them, but at night the animal
in their bodies overcame their reluctance
to be naked with each other,
and the mineral moon did its work.
At last when they woke up and were dead,
statues on their backs in the park,
they opened their mouths
and crawled out, pitifully soft and small,
not yet souls.

The Scar

Phrenologists and doctors know
beyond this symmetry of quartz-weight,
this living skull, yours, flourishes darkness.

A diabolical, queer knot of cells
has come to nest (large as a hummingbird
nest) behind your ear,

migrating from a lung.
When they took your skull apart,
it fit back perfectly, locking

like restored pyramids.
Your cobalt-treated head drops
gray flakes. You wear a wool cap

and worry the radiation's damaged hair-roots.
There is such little terror in your eyes,
though your brain outgrows itself.

Your memory outgrows itself:
all you have held and lost. Dragon
kimono and iridescent butterfly tray

from Japan you brought to a sweetheart.
Wartime memories *Esquire* nearly published.
A love affair in Detroit.

As you ask me to trace the scar,
I see a mark of wings, snow hieroglyphic,
mapping its possession, like moonlight

sometimes possessing the earth.
And, darkness outgrowing itself, a vanishing.
As I touch your milky head, you smile,

your eyes blue as the sky you will soon lose.

The Fearful Child

As a child I parleyed with animals, stuffed and real.
Making my kitten pilot of a boot, I guided
from one end of a string the dizzy flight and collapse.
I was fearful of people as well as things,
and my faithful toy shepherd with his painted face
sat by me on the bed in the gloom.
I was disdainful of dolls as weak people.

In the favorite story I told myself my parents
were made over into fair-limbed, brave angels
who smiled into their god's eyes when summoned.
I was benevolent, afraid to let go of this image
at night because I couldn't hide deep enough
under the covers to be overlooked by death,
the angel bending over me who had been wronged.

I read histories of queens, regal and barbarian,
whose leopard's eyes restrained man or wild beast.
I rambled along tidal rivers and in the marshes
where the green-golden grasses dazzled the sun,
and felt the ache of sea-air in my lungs.
I saw water spume near Atlantic cliffs.
I examined lichen. I saw great light drown darkness.

Then at thirteen I lay in the bleak bed before sleep
and heard the pleadings and the murderous kisses;
and burned, like a bear his fat, my soul.
I quaked at the sound of my voice whispering, *No*,
down the empty hallway to my parents' door,
or turned my face to the wall
and wept salt onto my knuckles.

In the serene light of sun-up, before sparrows
tumbled up from the earth, whispering and singing,
and the exquisite sea and sky mobilized
their heavy, blue currents, I was consoled.
I walked through beauty without knowing why
and told no one, wanting nothing else to touch me
and never to move anyone in any way.

I hid away from the house and learned the dark
was not a dream but could show the pale gravel
of a real driveway. I saw for the first time
later the new moon and the full moon
in one piece. I no longer feared the night,
night like a bear at ease in his wide habitat.
In the greatness of such space I said, *This is me.*

The Heron

A woman and her children are on a lake.
The woman steadies a rowboat
by bracing her legs against the bulkheads
and with oars that are like extensions
of her arms, as if there were no boat,
and she stood in twenty feet of water.
Each time one of her children jumps off,
she is rocked back a few feet.
The lake's shades of blue are interlarded
with cool whites and greens, but the woman's eyes
instead of reflecting the water
are as clearly blue as the open air,
as if she sees without shadows,
her gaze quiet and reaching as a formation
of birds. And when the younger child
says that she is too far away, she scolds him,
saying she will never leave him
alone out there, that all he has to do
is flutter-kick a little stronger. That evening,
on shore, his face small and white
like the ivory back of a hand mirror,
he asks her outside to see the blue heron.
They watch it descend in slow spirals
until it is lost against the dark pines,
and they must imagine its flight,
which might seem to him like a drawn-out
song of parting, each level a lower note,
the last a small white finale of water
and to her a darkening hunt
for fish and frogs. It depends on her look.
Nothing else will tell him.

She wants to stay there and not break
the silence, not look like anything
until he answers his questions,
like taking himself in his own arms,
remembering a time so solid
he could stand in the dissolving
day we know no more of than going.

Autumn Apology

Already the land is starting to forget gardens.
The dew, no longer sweet, glazes the latticed woods
with an unreal brilliance,
so the eyes must be shielded.
Reminiscences no longer hold the heart completely,
as someone held me a little roughly
once in somber deep groves.
Gold and silver lacquers
can't jail leaves in trees or warmth in the air.
The touch I was utterly dissolute to,
that caused collapse behind my knees,
sunslides in the lake,
is unconjurable.
Bits of the world, leaves, songs
scatter in painted light.
The days
change.

Aubade of an Early Homo Sapiens

—like none other before

In this lonely, varying light
of dawn with the residue of desire
like mist departing, I am walking.
Was it in your eyes, where my elongated face shone,
I saw for the first time,
as if all the transparent fire in these trees
had become palpable,
a hunger that was not wholly animal?

The need to tremble like dogwood, feeling the rain touch
   down.
My strange blood rises, and I may
see you, fair leaves slipping over you, half-hidden
in the morning. With the beasts
beside a pond, I conjure the inward sun
to leap into my brain. What remains?
Wild, beautiful petals all around.
A beast's face. And something, something else.

Stags and Salmon

(*Paleolithic drawing from the grotto of Lortet, France*)

A hint of fear
in the over-the-shoulder stare,
the mouth open not for chewing.
And hunters have come
to push the stags across the waters.
Of this succession,
bone and pearly space,
the artist caught
salmon like quarter moons
and placed them by the stags.
This is the drawing where
the beauty of relation begins.
A stag, carved round an antler,
turning its head, its antlers
crisp as flames,
and before it a running buck
crowded by salmon.
I think they must be swimming,
the lake water so clear
it cannot enter the design.

The Light Asks

It is a cold dawning and remarkably light out,
like from bed in his childhood, windows down to the floor.
The trees are tight as candlesticks in a box,
candles for the special occasions.

Slinging his rifle more squarely,
he looks at the stark white toes of his boots,
then at the sky. High in an oak
the nest of a large bird moves like an animal.

He walks to the dark circumference
of the tree, taps the trunk, and looks up it.
The coon is there, hugging a high limb.
His father told him to climb, and he climbs.

He'd had something like a dream once
when his parents were sleeping,
to paint his room, his bed, and his little brother
in the crib. Afterwards, the brush still

in his hand, he'd said a "cop"
told him he could paint, and he could.
He tests the branches with his hands and legs,
the dead ones the color of rake handles,

his eyes on the tree. When he looks up
for the coon, his mind slips,
and he falls like wood toward the roots.
His thigh wedges where a shaft of light had been.

His leg is foreign to him on impact;
and later when pain
comes like a stiff wind breaking through the woodlot
he tries to disown it. Every second

he pauses, deciding, light breaks away
from the far hills,
and he thinks, What now, Mom?
He watches the sunlight freeze on his thigh.

There are no answers in woodcraft
for this, and his father is not coming
to get him. Evening rolls out its dark carpet.
He faints.

When he wakes the light asks
who he is. The owls begin their calling in the silence.
He can't turn from the arms that hold him;
he thinks of the sweet peace of sleep.

No one is there to whisper him awake
until he is too deep in himself to be called to.
His rifle lies where it has fallen in snow.
Above him, light moves as branches.

The New Dog: Variations on a Text by Jules Laforgue

I.

The new dog's sugary breath warms my neck,
milkflecks on his muzzle.
Day begins, lighting his lavender eyes.
Relaxed as a child he seems to look
out across the yard at the sun's ascent.

The hour of last dreams when the bare elm
is tinged with gold. With this dog Max
I look out across the yard. I think
of newborn everywhere.
I think of Max who will wander
with curiously human eyes in the roses;
then imagine myself coming out of the garden,
going in place of Max to the road
and walking under a car.

I imagine entering this grave:
the full weight of Max counterposed against
the glance he turned away.

II.

You shovel the graveyard dirt too far
as if it were obscene to dig
a hole for Max, who is lying there
beside the rose bower, his ribs
and heart unstirred, his eyes
wide-open, tinged by the sunrise.

The hour of reverie when the elm
is lit with gold. The day begins.
Think of Max in another realm
too remote for touch, wandering in
a garden. Think of his dark eyeball
surveying darkness for us all.

Now the grave must be
refilled with the full weight of Max.
Beyond the sky's blue filigree
you cannot see the zodiac
when with sunlight in the air
you cover up his final stare.

Packing Mother's Things

I put into a carton the unstrung doll
wrapped in a baby quilt
whose eyes open and shut with a thunk
as the lids strike the molded brow
with the resonance of a hammer inside a clock.
I also put in an old radio,
shaped like the grille of a late model car,
whose singers sang *O Careless Love*
and *Lulu's Back in Town*.
Then I put in the inedible cake
and the tiny wax couple all in black.
Then the cameo. In the cameo a woman is etched
in shell, four folds to her skirt,
and she is holding one fold as she steps
and waves goodbye. The sky is abalone.
The two faintly Chinese buildings have a window
for looking out and a door for welcome.
But the woman, white as a cemetery in snow,
inaudible as a saved letter in a secret compartment
of a desk, is bidding goodbye.
I call the Goodwill and say
that they can have everything else.
But they won't take the windows, the doors,
the bathroom and the lawn;
they slide the mattresses down the stairs.
They are incredulous that I would leave
her shag rug red as cabbage, an aviary,
a homemade bookcase.
One of them finds a piece of scrap paper
and says, This is someone's,
don't you want it, I think it's a poem.

For the Infant Whose Heart Stopped for Eleven Minutes

Her heart soon fell as fast
asleep as the bobolink
who's here and then is past
before the sun's last wink.
Breathe for her. Wake her,
a pretty bird on the ground,
not say she'll come no more
peeping along the wind,
see nothing but mossy space
if ever she open her eyes.
Give her a little voice
that knows its melodies
among all windplayers
leaning over their songs,
lovelier and graver
after each night's passing.
And let her drift aloft,
tuned to the foremost wind
here scarcely heard, the soft
surging of the mind.
Give her fledgling wings
to span the natural
distances, and bring
her past the stone wall
where she has stopped to hear,
perhaps, dreamsongs of the lost
call down the twilit air;
the spirit songs of dust.

Unfinished Song

All day long, before the sun sings a requiem,
I walk through the thicket-rich hills
along deer paths where the finely cleft hooves
make wells in the mud, and the peace of mind
of water under grasses is sung quietly.
The green smell of grass and water rises.
And a tympani of savannah sparrows
plays in the glazed trees.
All day long, all along a stream
mottled with shadows,
whose pulse is felt in the wood finger
dancing at the surface, through lyric hollows,
each different from the last, fish like pebbles
piling on each other.
All day long, intoxicated by odors and songs
of damp earth, the soft panting
of earth's withers,
I walk to forget
the simplest song,
lips scarcely parted,
the last note of lament unfinished:

Is there a solitude greater
than the solitude of snow cast into water
like a dress cast down?
Only the moon, and the naked body
dragging itself along the ground
then stooping to kiss, darkly, itself
for the last time.

Old Cat

In her sleep she makes a human sound,
god-awful, tame. She gets
the fish and milk she needs,
so it seems to her there's no sensation
in the world, no jaw of sunlight
on the woodpigeon's breast.
Just sometimes in the great loll
of her fatigue, she flexes her sinews
and sharpens her claws on the curtain,
a helix of strength. Then does
the downpour of birds outdoors get in
the shell of her cat eyes, really?
Or does it lag below sense, ceasing
along benumbed nerves to be,
like spectres without moisture or freshness
or the pieces of things thrown to her
she can't see?

An Adolescent Girl

The girl who's looking for love
and is afraid of the rites
is walking in the forest.
Birds are mating
in a dance above her head.
Spiders leave their froth
in the wild flowers,
and she doesn't know what it is.
The little acts of violence
in the woods startle her,
but the fragrant decay of an animal
is almost pleasant,
its sun-melted body
sprouting greener grass, the small
cathedral of bones absorbed.
For a long time she cannot move
further into or away from the hot garden.

The savory light wakes her.
Bits of the forest
have been rubbing their colors
on her skirt.
She walks, under the trees
like statues
set in a slow gesture of longing,
toward home. The air laurels
ever so lightly her hair;
the boys may smell
the frail, wild beauty there.

Country Marriage

They married out of school
when she could feel the baby's feet
fixed deep inside and feel
her passion quicken for the sweet

romance. He bought on time
a trailer on an ugly hill
and worked in town sometimes.
She leaned her forehead on the sill

and watched him tune the car
and vowed she cared for living things.
She saw how everywhere
the pollen cast its nets and strong

buds splashed a little color
onto the waving greenery,
then didn't mind the squalor
of axles, oil pans, grease, and flies.

She loved the honeysuckle,
the running light across the land;
she made herself a necklet
and spoke to him in tones of lead.

A quick in time, a bead
of blood, and dumb imaginings
became their solitude.
Their yard filled up with junk and rings

of rainbow in the ditch
they got their drinking water from.
She didn't care so much.
She didn't care if he stayed home.

When summer turned to ash
a little witless sheep was born,
child slow to be itself
which lay in a crib all alone

caught up in their neglect.
She saw the bitter apple tree
and gutted car perfect
in winterfall, and senselessly

an equilibrium
held them something like love that year.
The child held in its arms
a sour doll. They had come far.

Passage

Held off and drawn by ordinary
differences, as if a lens were pushed
out of focus, or the diverging blue threads
on a map were the directions of impatience,
I tell myself,

here is a raven, yellow beak,
ringed eyes, sleek, in the graveyard
grown so tame for crumbs, its predecessor
lies under a country verse.

Let your giving-looks, like the sameness
of prize orchids, breed or wither
in their own season.
I remember snow in May—
breath after breath of petals
strewed the ground.
Our eyes could not unmake it.

The only fidelity
is in our fingertips tracing
and retracing the exact passage of the veins
of the throat. And love, once spoken,
comes with a wing held over the heart.

Our Night

Deep in the night, the desk
and armchair dim guardians,
no sound but the peaceful breathing
of ourselves,

we begin slowly to make love,
touching each other everywhere water
bathes the rose.

When my cries are borne gently
on the dark air and fall,

I wonder, is this the last time?

Two Poems / Toward Silence

I. AS I SLEPT

Moment by hopeless moment
you stared at my relaxed stranger's face.
Of the wind's rattle, and tumult of sea
mounting the esplanade,
that failed to rouse me,
you thought only it was time to go.
I woke before you crossed the muffled floor,
and saw the prison of your eyes,
gray and set, no gesture of love unlocks.
And as the storm leaked in the spaces,
scarcely aloud you said my name,
goodbye. Then. Nothing
but the click of the downstairs door.

II. YOUR LETTER

   . . .our bodies
without intercession of word or thought,
you write.
               Out the window
the trees are clotting light; their scripts
across the snow disclose no meaning,
yet pose the shifting of moments
toward June. And beneath the snow
no equivalents for flowers: Ox-Eye,
Bleeding Heart, Our-Lord's-Candle.
I cannot ever touch you and not want to ask
your name for this possession,
something like light caged in snow, and heat.
I cannot bear your answer
and cannot come there.

Frost

The days are getting shorter, you said.
You uproot burr and mallow, make a space
against the knotted weeds that interlace
like textile. Autumn sews with slenderest thread.
You said it like goodbye, as if tonight
the owl would leave his plumage on the ground.
The sun goes down and the late-coming wind
lifts, unraveling the ends of light
on the horizon. Helmeted by dusk,
you walk toward me holding tomato vines
to hang inside the window. There'll be time
enough for this last fruit to ripen. Hush,
you say, listen—with muffled wing the night
nears; the morning frost will feather light.

Death in Winter

Dropped in straw
in a barn lagged against winter,
the lamb had vertigo.
With no malice the lamb's mother

moved away.
The lamb hobbled and bleated in dark
cold sanctuary,
knelt like a monk, then stepped crooked

toward crooked light.
It leapt through the torn boards without
fear or deliberate
reflection. In its eyes the slight

snow threshold
had blazed like some beheld heaven.
Then deepening cold
and ice grown in its eyes like stone.

Great snow fell
onto soughing trees. Softly
snow stroked the curly wool.
A balm of snow swept in mercy.

The lamb's gaze,
rolled in, envisioned all sweetness
and lasting light: the brain's
pure honeycomb had crystallized.

The Cemetery Is Empty

The stones are streaked
as if a community had stood
and wept away all cause for tears.
Verses, names have rained into graves,
and the pain has come apart
like a very old doll in the finder's hands.

The Garden

Before fruit and insect to mar the fruit,
I stand in the bare loam
up to my ankles, hoeing,
hoeing the black sea
until my body revels in the salt-drench
and fatigue of making black blacker,
and I'm gradually pulling in the net that is night.
Then the peas are in,
and it is night. I undress
and lie down like moonlight in the garden,
dying as simply as I can.

The Embroidery

Grandmother embroiders the summer day.
She sits amid the bodies and light of childhood,
lilac-scented, perspiring,

sewing life-like flora in cloth the color of cream.
Pollen is strewn in the air;
some spices her hair.

The design on the porch sofa isn't far off
from the green and golden scene,
a water-garden, she inextricably sews into new cloth.

To look at her face, you would not see birth or death,
but even as hands stitch the fictitious daylight,
a drop of her blood like dew forms

and falls among the mass of raised flowers.
For a second she looks perplexed; you see both.
She sucks her finger, and brushing it on her apron

continues. A pitcher of lemonade
is on the table, a parakeet clatters in its ornate cage,
and mildew casts its net around.

The Winter without Snow

The man carried bucket after bucket of plaster dust
up the earthen ramp of the barn that caught fire
and emptied each as if he were dumping snow
onto the blackened beams.
In the trees there were little glass seeds,
souvenirs of winter without snow.

When the man turned back toward the house,
he wore a helmet of dusty mother-of-pearl,
and his eyelashes were silvery half-moons.
I watched him with all the coldness I had,
yet it would not snow.

Nothing could make it snow.
Not the burst water pipes, the leggings,
the sleds, or the white horses.
Not the smoky fountains, the clouds.
They were souvenirs of winter without snow,
as was my wish for a white field
like a fresh beginning.

A Good Cafeteria

The half-daft lady at the counter
won't eat anything with her pork loin.

Every five minutes
a waitress says to her: "A nice salad."
"Perhaps tea." And finally the lady
wants a little cottage cheese.

Outdoors the eerie snowflakes:
pieces of snowmen
falling away quietly.

The Secret

Night's made a ground nest,
laid its eggs, then disappeared.
I've come upon the eggs this morning
beyond the border of the garden.

Strokes, straws, wisps and coils
litter the grass around the cache,
tokens of a single skirmish,
perhaps, in this dangerous place.

Kneeling, I can only
marvel that the eggs are whole
as little earths spinning in miles
of nothing, clarified by sunlight.

Each egg is delicate
with specks and soaked with gray dew.
Inside the garden morning's hound sees
me and leaps at the end of his chain.

Shall I gather these
brown eggs and take them into
the kitchen? Light throngs in the grasses,
and soon their hiding place will be found.

The Daughter

In the close-pressed shadows
any whisper was a china figure falling,
the dress and limbs
to be picked up by anyone: she implored him
not to wake his daughter.
He lurched away
and she looked at her half sister.
Or was she looking at the swift-as-flight
image of herself transfiguring?
She never speaks of this
but goes like others
as if absorbed in a ceremony.
While her face is glazed by unconcern,
might she not be the china maiden
bowing still on the dresser?

Three Apparitions

*Et, comme un oeil naissant couvert par ses paupieres
Un pur esprit s'accroit sous l'ecorce des pierres!*
                                    NERVAL

I. CRABAPPLE

In rain the crabapple,
frazzled with thorns,
struggles to weep.

Tears begin
down the pale bark,
fatten and roll

to the tips, and every
time, spring-clear
and hard, one falls,

it's caught on
another bough,
impaled, often,

on the point of a thorn.
You'll see each break
and fall again

and also see,
if you're quick, three
or even four

tear-beads on a thorn,
as if the tree
wore gems to grieve.

Drop by drop
the superb tears
fall on marrow-

piercing thorns. Is it rain
or is it sap,
crabapple tree?

II. STONE IN THE SHAPE OF A TORSO

This Eve cannot wholly waken,
yet in her dream her breast of stone,
pink-embossed, spattered with lichen,
is made of sighs so delicate
the wings of hummingbirds escape,
whose soft ascending shadows won't be back.
In ballet light she sleeps.
Granite wrestles on her torso,
and an exhaling and breathing of wind
stirs the saffron-colored grasses near her ribs.
As the eyelid hides the nascent eye
(as if it has to take form to be),
her spirit grows against the stone.
Still no one speaks the word to waken.
Forever she feels the inside of stone
lean to a breeze. Forever dreams
the hatches of light called firmament.

III. DEER

The field of puffballs is egg-white.
A deer made the wind gush at her knee,
freeing like seraphim the spores.

Influenza

A rubber girl is living
in my body, not like a doll
or dead person or soul (things which have no pulse)
because I feel a new pulse intruding
when I try to raise my head.

The rubber girl has copied my muscles
and bones imperfectly
and inhabits me with a sack of sponges
or a bag of eggs.

As afternoon weakens
to a vapor, her will in me
to lie as a shape inside a dress
breaks my solitude into beads of sweat.
I awake angrily to the languors

of the sickroom. Drawn shades,
swarms of gray light
in the mediciney air, and terrible,
not from me, a welling-up desire
to cry and cry.

A Red Nightgown

I see in your eyes a red nightgown
and, in slow increase,
as if you stand in the doorway of a house
in the warm sun, or the recollection of a dawn
stirred some reflection in my look,
the desire to push to one side
oaths and bonds. This woman's body
has worn like another body
the reddened silk
and known by tomorrow's dawn
nothing changes—the sun's instinct
to roll across the sky and the bitter shining
of memories at each threshold.
It's as if all we knew was letting
the sun warm our bodies
and play on our faces.
Let's go indoors
where the light is not so remarkable
and relax. The walls are barely apparent,
the ceiling a shadow, the bed smooth and sleeping.
Nothing here that time or sun will waken.
Shall we begin?

What Will Become of the Fat and Slow Performing Woman?

There in the tutu—
                melons, bear-
fat: where her beauty has gone.
Stripped to her youth, she was
an exotic dancer. Bones pliant as air,
she performed the arch and counter-arch
above circus cages, tethered by her hair.
Men lay down in their lives for her.

Cow-heavy, burying her chair,
she preens for her old audience.
What's to become of her,
her face aswim with golden fats,
thighs massive with taboos?
Her laughter bulldozes
away all sympathy from the side-show air.
Hah! What's to become of you?

Sometimes We Say It Is Love

for my brother

Sometimes we say it is love as one says now—
that we wrestle as a man and woman
learning not to hurt each other.
Because the heart cannot tell us why.
We think we are alone: we look in
room after room with eyes and door keys,
with ears and mirrors,
but find only what we knew to begin with:
something wakes, something stumbles into its shadow.
Then we call it hate, feeling we want
to knock someone down, or just
slap someone hard across the face.
We feel it the way we feel someone's eyes
through a window, the way silence strikes.
Little by little we become alone.
We want to know each other's limbs
and rib cage like we know our own.
We hold each other against the floor.
We bruise. As if we could transfix the body,
fill it to the brim with ourselves,
and it would never forget us:
we might wake one morning with dread
like lungs filled with cotton,
and someone else would breathe for us;
our hearts hollow, and another
heart consent to take their shape;
unable to feel, and someone's hands
draw the dark moon out of our brains.

To Fish

1.

The path smells like mushrooms, hint of dusk.
Crabapples, briars, tinged by sunlight,
waver like static before birdsong;
deliciously bitter the green bud.
In the river's glistening dusk
trout thread behind the elongated worm,
then disappear in windshift,
in an overlay of April chromes.
When one is hooked
it splatters me lightly with water.
Through the gills I put a stick
so it's weighted to the river bank.
Deer-fall, and resin on tree trunks.
Me in last glaze feeling the air
curl across the darkening water.
And the pulp, still pink, on my hands
I wipe on the bark of a birch tree,
then bend again, stock-still, over the river
until forest shade reaches the bottom.
Alder leaves tremble like sighs.
Birdsongs fall asleep. Having no image
dark enough for the dark current,
no glint of trout flipping sideways
to a drowned log, I walk home.
Only upper branches are lit,
and the last sounds are the crickets.

2.

At home a medley of welcome
and "When do we eat?" The table's set.
I flick a fisheye from my shirt
and hand over seven to be gutted.
One still yawns, as if for more air.
The kitchen smells of butter.
We begin to eat, the April water
flavoring the meat that lifts
easily off the ribs and spine.
Not all the trout
swimming in the river or arranged
nicely on a platter with parsley and lemon
could alter the silence at the table.

Cold Frame

Stray ends of light in the window
glimmer into a wan mosaic of my face,
the translucent forehead pressed on the pane.
I see through the delicate siege
of this ghost, visitor and visitant,
knowing darkness will take it back again,
a plum-colored haze wreathing the bushes,
and, just beyond the hedgerow in the yard,
snowfall blowing like torn parchment.

Apple blossoms are falling,
making a sour lyric of the snow,
and though green wavers of light
rise from the dooryard like spring,
this slant of drifting grains of ice,
like little crystal minutes, obscures
in gray weather the frail shoots.
Here I am again in winter;
the snow piles up on the window sill.

Underneath the roof of the chicken house
the soil simmered—paramoecia and melted
snow—but in such mildness as of dreams
that remind me in the mornings of something
not unpleasant and not totally formed.
On a day like this one, the unexpected
weight of snow caved in the chicken house,
and the ground next August
was a cornucopia of green weeds.

In a concentrated drop of distance
a robin makes a bickering dance on snow,
but nothing happens. The false weather
is brilliant in the light it sheds:
the hot-house snow protects the seedlings,
their soft, vagrant tangle. The hair-spring
work of the deepest cells continues,
as if an unseen clock hung in the air.
The light always comes back.

His Mind Ceases

His mind ceases to prowl with you in the blue underbrush
where the vague and changing shapes
of your playthings lie carelessly.
In the darkness with you his sighs and quick breast-heavings
come familiar. You know your brother sleeps.
You lie under the cloudy ceiling of nighttime and listen,
tense and sullen,
for the slippered treading of a ghost.
Days your brother comes clutching at your sleeve,
a nuisance; and now the dismantled room
thick with shadows, he's safe asleep.
Down the dark lanes you go
and cannot sleep.
You'll wander miles before you let the darkness in,
your body inert in surrender,
all the playthings heaped on your bed as if for barter
with whomever you might meet out there,
your face turned generously to your brother,
who will awaken you
and tell you the story of his dreams first.

Prayer for My Son

My thinking that you could lie in my hands
quietly, makes it so.
You become my whispered words, almost
a prayer in my interlocking hands.

So little of what
I see is what you are. Fingernails,
cartilage, cell deaths, layers of skin,
and the garden in your head:
wild pig, the air's dragons,

a humming thick as honey just below sense
and the picked castles of bone
which held essences once, and still do. There,
the animals look at you as if you were an angel,
which is to say they will not look.

Your sleeping head heavy on my lap,
the flower of your ear tilted
in involuntary sunlight,
I ask that it could be so

for you to waken day after day
like a traveler: lonely as you'll always be,
tired, beaten, perhaps,
but smiling with ease
and a little in awe of everything.

The Day of the Body

I. IF A MODEL

If a model is posed by a sunny window
and the artist is in love with light,
he draws the white white vitals
of her body in sweeping unbroken curves
as if she were made of threads,
but if the artist is in love with flesh
and wishes to remain chaste,
she possesses for him all her animal beauty
in a belly and hips that are lit
as if by wingfuls of warm air
a day-sparrow caught in the sheaves.

II. SHE THINKS OF LOVE

Wanting to suggest a wild and luxuriant soul
and her dignity, she molds her body
after Eve's. She sees herself
by a shaded brook; a dark purple road
and green foreground, where she
undresses. She looks at her belly,
then presses there with her hand open
until she can press no more,
and the ridges of fatty tissue
between her fingers are just fat enough.
Then, like Eve, she puts on
her lips an ironic smile
and lies down and thinks of love
which means of someone she has seen.

III. THE MAN AND THE WOMAN

The man and the woman
have been getting to know each other,
and now they are going to make love.
The bed represents the unlighted parts
of a picture and their desire
seems to act as a wandering beam of light
that weaves around their thighs.
His hand defines the turning of her hips
just as her hips make his hands
their reality. Whether like tree trunks
or earth or light-filled air,
their bodies are caught up in a feeling
they do not quite understand: Four dark
eyes surprised by each other in a room.

IV. SO WHEN HE LEAVES

They aren't violent, so when he leaves
in the middle of the night
he says, tomorrow morning will be
like any other morning. He leaves her
lying on a light chrome-yellow sheet
only slightly indecent, as if she's bathed
in lamplight. After falling asleep
she sees a native girl on her belly,
showing a portion of her frightened face.
The background is purple,
a color of terror, but in the dream
she cannot tell what the girl is afraid of.
Perhaps she is thinking of someone dead
or that death is thinking of her.

V. WHERE ARE YOU GOING?

The looser his skin gets
the more he gets used to his soul
flying in a frequently squalid room
like a bird. All the windows are closed
and he is the child who ducks
each time the bird whirs by. With every fiber
the child wants to free the sparrow,
there is strain around his eyes,
but it will not light, and to the boy
the bird is unpredictable, may change
its circular flight and crash into his head.
Sooner or later, the boy will be brave
and rush to the door and open it.
"Where are you going?" the boy will call,
and the bird may sing, but no answer.
The boy will become a white dot
in a field and the bird a vapor.

No Batter

Dark-faced at home plate
your son with a chicken stance
and taped thumb pops a foul
over the dugout

where the other team chants
"nobadder, nobadder"
onto the hood of the blue Chevy
like the son who worked carnivals

pounding the stakes in summer
and forgetting to switch off
the helical gears
when ten rode in a cab

in a dizzy oval
or someone on beer
who busted into Hobbs' Garage
and took nothing. Someone

feels around the gully
the hardball made
like the dented road sign
someone shot at from far off

and the dog's hip
that partially healed
after a deer-lover's slug
just crossed the corn fields

and sank in.
A man shouts,
"Straighten 'er out!"
and points to the plywood fence

over the fielder's head
as a cousin with a rifle
points to the dark stand of pines
twitching with sinews

and eyes
of a 10-point buck
as your son scuffs the dirt,
raises his hands nearly over his head,

sticks out his skinny butt
and freezes, like one who might
swing and miss
and sit down hard.

Ode to the Horseshoe Crab

Dullest of all creatures, the horseshoe crab
crawls with its brethren to the beach at low tide;
they are broad-backed with muck-colored plates
and out of water look like stones.

Boys who wouldn't torture anything higher,
torture these crabs, which have nothing
that could be called real eyes, their bland backs
suggesting the faces of idiots.

They have no enthusiasms, and can't move fast.
Their undersides are full of twiddling legs
and leaf-like gills. *Limulus polyphemus*
has a low sex drive.

Commonly, boys crack the crabs with stones,
large ones that the back can't bear,
and something that looks like brains,
a gray tapioca that smells sweet, comes out.

Having no capacity for love or thought,
they trudge in the salty tide, swallowing small forms
of marine life. In 350 million years the sun
has failed to break their sleep, the sleep before being born.

Constellation

Again the lilacs
smell like new decay.
Here in the living room
and out on the bushes

the white and purple
stars spoil in clusters,
reminding of curdled
milk and blood's platelets

which some people drink,
plugging a cow's vein
and draining one udder
for nourishment. A death

is only beautiful
if we concentrate
on distances, neither
east nor south, but somewhere

through vegetation
of lights and small pools
where the fatted lilacs
echo the stars' ferment.

The Homemade Piano

The minstrel peers through tiny eyeglasses
the size of tears at Bach
and with fantastic concentration reduces
the grand scale to fit his homemade piano—
a melancholy squeezed down from his brow
to say, "Yes, I have enough," or "No,
I haven't enough."

He wags his fingers up and down like sticks
fastened with a hinge to the knuckles,
but his music
stays in the passerby's head
like the sense of heaviness in the hand
though a pail being carried home
is half-spilled.

In the polyphony of one little keyed instrument
there are remembered perfumes, caesuras,
and the oriole whose vowels
bewilder each morning with fortunate
and unfortunate decrees.
A rustle moves through the audience.
Here on a homemade piano is the empty heart

and full heart in counterpoint.
Tomorrow the minstrel will set
his simple box on another street corner.
If his strain still haunts,
you may find him there and ask him
why his song has no ending
and why so lovely. He'll play the variations.

AFTERWORD

We must face the dread reality of nuclear death, which is not the sum of so many individual deaths, but an infinity of death. Believing that no one knows for certain whether a nuclear war will follow the scripts our strategists and generals have written or that total extinction is remote closes the mind's eyes and stops up its mouth. Neither the immaculate rhetoric of men in their pin-striped suits and uniforms nor a couple of planks and three feet of dirt will save us; only, perhaps, to recognize the conspiracy between us to call death by lesser names, not the infinite black above and below us with no least heartbeat, no thread of air.

Carol Frost was born in Lowell, Massachusetts in 1948. She studied at the Sorbonne, the State University of New York, Oneonta, and Syracuse University. She has taught at Syracuse University, and now teaches at Hartwick College. A chapbook, *The Salt Lesson*, was published in 1976 by Graywolf Press. Her first full-length book, *Liar's Dice*, was the Elliston Committee's sole honorable mention in 1978. She has also published a second chapbook, *Cold Frame* (1982). She is the recipient of fellowships in poetry from the National Endowment for the Arts, Yaddo, Bread Loaf Writers' Conference, and Syracuse University. She is married and has two sons, Daniel and Joel.